WIDOWS:
Women of Courage

A Biblical Look at Widows
From God's Perspective

by
LYNDA ROBINSON

15 14 13 12   8 7 6 5 4 3 2 1

Widows: Women of Courage—A Biblical Look at Widows From God's Perspective

ISBN 13: 978-1-937250-03-4

Copyright © 2012 by Lynda Robinson
Published by Paige1Publishing
Tulsa, OK | Nashville, TN

918.706.4359 | www.paige1publishing.com

Acknowledgements

My heartfelt thanks goes to Jan Fields who spent hours arranging all the information I gave her into book form and to Jayne Sleeter who so graciously directed my steps through the publishing process. Also, I want to thank Pastor Mark Brazee and Pastor Hayne Schurz, who both encouraged me to put this information in book form. My thanks as well to all my dear friends, some who shared their own stories of widowhood with me, and those who prayed, encouraged, and loved me.

Contents

Acknowledgements..iii

Preface..vii

1 Beginning Again..1

2 Heaven's Plan...5

3 Heaven's Provision 13

4 Biblical Examples...21

5 Heaven's Promises..31

    * God Provides Material Needs

    * God Provides Favor/Blessing

    * God Is a Companion/Helper

    * God Brings Peace and Sleep

    * God Is Healer—Body and Soul

    * God Is Your Protector

6 Overcoming Hurt and Bitterness...43

    "A Mandate Before New Destiny Emerges"

7 Victory in the Word...51

    "Deliverance from Grief by God's Word"

8 Master Keys to a New Life...59

    * Salvation

    * Holy Spirit, the Comforter

    * Prayer and the Word of God

    * Other People

9 Scriptures to Pray.. 67

    * Promises Given by God for Widows
    * Blessings to People Helping Widows
    * Curses to People Refusing Help to Widows
    * Widows' New Covenant Responsibilities

10 Practical Helps 79

11 A New Day Dawning 81

Prayer of Salvation 83

Prayer to be Baptized in the Holy Spirit 85

About the Author 87

Endnotes 88

Preface

Widows: Women of Courage is a *new destiny* for me. Birthed through my own personal experiences, this book is written to bring restoration and deliverance to other widows facing similar issues and needing real answers.

If you have lost your husband through death, you know it takes courage to even face the day. Widowhood involves new ways of living in every area of your life. The old comfortable ways are gone forever, and new ways of life and living are required by the circumstances. You have entered a time of life called change and it is change that no one wants to make. At any age becoming a widow is a new frontier in life when you are certainly not looking to face new frontiers—especially alone.

In my journey of challenges and victory, God deposited His Words into my heart, mind, and life—but not just for me. This book is for you. My hope is you will gain a new perspective as to what God has for you and overcome in every situation as you read and apply the Word of God to your life. God has not deserted you, and He has made provision for your future to come alive again!

CHAPTER 1

Beginning Again

The Old Testament relates an account of widows in the Book of Ruth that emphasizes God's concern. The providence of God and the blessing Ruth finds in her future husband Boaz are highlighted as they fall in love and create a marriage made in heaven. However, the Book of Ruth would not be possible without Naomi, her mother-in-law. The part to spotlight for our purposes has more to do with Naomi, and her side of the story. Actually both Ruth and Naomi, and the seldom mentioned sister-in-law of Ruth, are all widows at the onset. The sister-in-law chooses stay behind when Naomi determines to return to her home, leaving Naomi and Ruth as the focus of the story.

In the Book of Ruth we see a panorama view of widowhood. The picture of the courage required and obstacles to be overcome are more viewable from Naomi's perspective than from Ruth's. Naomi lost not only her husband but both sons. In Naomi's Jewish culture women had few rights and privileges. It is quite a contrast from 21st Century America. The only things left to Naomi were her two daughters-in-law. So Naomi decided her only option was to return to her family in Bethlehem where things were better. She told both of the girls to go back to their own families but Ruth refused to leave her side! We will go into greater detail about Ruth later but for now, know there are several promises and provisions of God in this book that are replete throughout the Bible for every widow.

God's Specific Promises for Widows

In His Word, God promises to take care of widows. If you are a Christian and widowed, God is here for you. You have to arise from your sense of loss to look for the victorious plan He has for you. It takes courage to overcome and get on the other side of widowhood. The death of a husband before the appointed lifespan of man has the sensation of great loss in so many ways. However, a woman of faith, a believer, a Christian, who has trusted her life to Jesus Christ, has an empowerment, an enablement, an anointing from heaven in Almighty God, the very Creator of the universe. A person of faith, or believer, is enabled to overcome in every circumstance of life, including the death of a husband. God has made provision for His children in every arena of life. His provisions cover every aspect and season of life, and the loss of a husband is especially noted in the Scriptures. His love for women, specifically the widow and the fatherless, is seen from the Word of God, which we will see step-by-step.

This book is a result of my own personal grief and recovery from the loss of my husband, Fred. We were married for more than 47 years, and he was greatly loved by me, our children, and grandchildren. In the midst of my own grief, God brought His Word to me, giving me peace, encouragement, and consolation no person could have offered. You may find as I did that for a while friends and family are available to you, but then the moments of despair, anger, looming decisions, bills, and an unknown future must be faced. No one is there to help, or so it would seem. If you will turn to God, He will, in His Word, as your Father, come to you personally and supply answers for every problem you face. Know of a certainty God has abundant answers and provisions for every need of your life. My desire in this book is to reveal *God's* answers. It is through God's Word I gained my own victory. From the Bible, cover to cover, the Holy Spirit opened the eyes of my heart and mind (Ephesians 1:16-21) to His super-natural help in every realm of life—spiritual, emotional, financial, relational, and physical. God ministers to the whole person—not just one area of life. God takes personal responsibility for widows as we will see through His promises in the Bible. His very Words are there for you to read and embrace. Study, meditate, and stand upon the Word of God in every circumstance that comes.

God the Creator of the universe will become your:

- Husband

- Provider

- Protector

- Deliverer

- Friend

- Emotional Support

- And much, much more.

Trusting God

The Bible says God's provision depends on our "trust" and confidence in Him, our Heavenly Father, just as it does for a wife in a marital relationship. Proverbs 3:5-6 says, "Trust in the Lord with *all* thine heart; lean not unto thine own understanding. But in all your ways acknowledge Him and He shall direct thy paths" (emphasis mine). Direction, aid, and assistance are available at the time of widowhood from your Heavenly Father. You may feel abandoned, without provision, alone, scared, uncertain, fearful, untrusting, or incapable. You need Him to take your hand in His, put His loving arms around you, and take you to the land of the living from the land of darkness, depression, and grief. Your Heavenly Father is ready to do that!

This book is not simply my story as a widow who lost her husband—an abandoned woman left alone to fend for herself. Absolutely not! We have a Father God Who wants to supply our every need according to His resources and riches in heaven (Phil. 4:19). In fact, God wants to do this for every believer—single, married, or widowed—but it is often in desperation, when it looks like our world is crumbling and falling apart, that we turn to God, or at least turn to someone or something outside of our resources since we have exhausted all other options.

If you are ready to embrace solutions, rekindle courage, and begin the new destiny your Father has just for you, come with me on this journey through the Word of God and watch yourself transform!

CHAPTER 2

Heaven's Plan

Fred, my wonderful husband of over 47 years, had been ill for several years. I was confident I was prepared to face his death and passing away. As much as I thought I was prepared, I was not…. As you already know—if you are a widow reading this book—there are so many decisions to make, things to do, and important matters to be considered during a very unstable and emotional time. During these trying moments you are forced not only to *think* about these challenging decisions but you have to *face* them.

It would seem, right when I thought I was getting a handle on matters and things were beginning to straighten out, I would get another phone call or piece of mail that would have to be resolved.

In the midst of these troubling times soon after my husband's death, the Lord told me to set aside time with Him. I was impressed in my spirit to come aside with Him and to look in the Bible for what He has to say about widows. First of all, I didn't know He had said so much about widows. I knew a few passages, but as I began to run references from a concordance I found 83 different passages referencing widows, not including the Book of Ruth which is *all* about widows.

When God calls you away unto Himself and He gives you instructions, you know that life and blessings are on the way. Our God is a good and awesome God, Who has planned wonderful things for His children (Jer. 29:11). His words to me were, *Come to My Word. Let Me show you what I have for you and what I can do for you. I want to comfort you! I want to help you! I want to bless you!* There was something very special God had for me, and I had no idea how He would change my current as well as my future world. Through His Word, God has made that invitation to each and every person who will hear and obey, including you. I did not hear an audible voice. It was an inward voice—an inward witness or inward knowing. I followed, adhered, and obeyed!

It is my heart's desire to see widows comforted and encouraged by God's Word the way I was heartened, blessed, and helped when I became a widow. In Hebrews 13:8 the Bible says, "Jesus Christ the same yesterday, and today, and forever." God never does anything without purpose. He's always concerned about us as individuals and He also has plans to use us to build the Kingdom of God, ministering and touching others.

Romans 8:14 says, "For as many as are led by the Spirit of God, these are the sons of God" (NKJV). As a daughter of God, I was led by the Spirit of God to come aside from all of my busyness to hear what God had to say. The Bible is God's will to each of His kids. It's all about His promises, His provisions, and His plans for His children. The impression by the Holy Spirit in my spirit was to look up every Scripture in the Bible on widows. I took my Bible out (a new Bible that had hardly been used) and a pad of paper, a pencil or pen, some

Post-It Notes, and my *Strong's Concordance*, and I began to look up Scriptures on widows.

After locating all of the "widow" Scriptures, I counted them. I found there were 83 Scriptures on widows in the Word of God. I thought, *That's amazing! God really does have something to say about widows.* Finding these Scriptures brought courage and hope to me. I began to think perhaps I was not alone—perhaps God would work on my behalf—perhaps God had a future plan for me!

Hope for the Future

I started in the book of Beginnings, the Book of Genesis, and I read every Scripture on widows. Every time I found a passage regarding widows I pulled off a Post-It Note and placed it on that particular Scripture. I went through the entire Bible and noted all 83 Scriptures. You can imagine what my Bible looked like. I also found there were still more passages in the Bible on widows that didn't use the word "widows." For example, in the Book of Ruth, which we mentioned earlier, the whole book is about widows, but in the King James Version of the Bible it *never* mentions the word "widow." Also there are other widows referenced in Scripture not noted as "widows." After locating these Scriptures, I went back and reread each Scripture again. God supernaturally ministered encouragement, peace, and comfort to me. It is my heart cry and passion that the words in this book will produce hope, peace, encouragement, and comfort to you just as it did for me. I am praying the Spirit of Revelation will work in your heart as you listen with your heart. God has a special place in His Father heart for widows and for you specifically.

There are so many Scriptures where God expresses His plans and provision for widows; how they are to be treated; even the consequences of those who mistreat widows, who refuse to help aid or take care of them. There are passages telling what God expects of widows; and what they can accomplish in their life. In researching these Scriptures it gave hope for my future.

The Word of God produces courage. It produces hope. It produces strength. These are all characteristics needed to face the decisions, go new places, try new things, and do things differently than you've ever done them before. It takes courage and in God, you have the courage it takes to overcome, to triumph, to be a hero in your own life, and to begin again.

Without the help of God through His Word and the dependence upon Him through prayer and worship, sensing His presence, receiving His direction, and knowing His love and peace, I am not sure if I could have made it. But every step of the way I sensed His presence. Every day I continued to be aware of Him. Every second of every day I knew He was there. And He's still here with me, even now.

I can't help but praise God and give Him my thanks for always being there for me. But He's not just available for me, He's there for every widow who will make Him Savior and Lord of their life. He wants to be there to meet our needs, protect us, direct our children and grandchildren, and give us abundant life—to the full, till it overflows. That's our Savior and Lord, Jesus Christ!

As I began to research the word "widow" in the Bible, I began to realize that some of the greatest miracles in the Bible were for widows. Glory to God! He's there for me! Discovering these miracles helped me to understand how the Father helps us. It gave me encouragement to know some of these women in Scripture had potential disasters much worse than what was going on in my life. God met their needs and if God met their needs, He will meet yours and mine.

Put God In Remembrance

In Isaiah 43:26, God says, "Put me in remembrance." In other words God is saying, *Tell Me what I promised you in My Word. I will surely do it!* Many Christians are waiting for God to "fix their problem" without putting Him in remembrance.

Evangelist John Wesley said that God does nothing unless a man prays.[1] When God creates the first man, Adam, He gives him authority over all the earth and everything in it (Gen. 1:28). But after a short while Adam disobeys God and refuses to use his authority when his wife, Eve, is tempted and eats of the fruit of good and evil (Gen. 3). Everything God does has purpose. When Adam commits high treason and sins, he basically gives all of his God-given authority to Satan. God in His foreknowledge knows the outcome—that Adam will sin—and has already, from the foundation of the earth, planned to send His Son Jesus to the earth to get His man back. This is accomplished when Jesus Christ comes into the earth and gives His life for the sins of humanity (John 3:16-17). Now because of Christ, the born-again man has authority in the earth, and God expects him to use it. God gave man, as a free-willed moral agent, authority and dominion over the earth, but once it was forfeited to Satan, God lost access to it (Luke 4:5-8). So the only way God has access in the earth is through a born-again man who knows his rights, his privileges, and his authority (Eph. 1:19-22).

When God says to "put Me in remembrance," He is saying, *remind Me of My Word so I can have access in the earth through you.* If we don't speak His Word through our prayer and confession, God doesn't have access in the earth. He gave that authority to His children. In order to receive what God promised, we must use God's Word, declare it to Him, and refuse to bow to circumstances that would contradict it. Prayer and confession are vital elements of our provision from God. We have to use our faith in God and His Word; then activate it with the words of our mouth.

Oftentimes when I get into a difficult situation, I will go back to these Scriptures in the Bible. I will put God in remembrance because He is no respecter of persons (Acts 10:34). *The Message* Bible translation says, "God plays no favorites! It makes no difference who you are or where you're from—if you want God and are ready to do as he says, the door is open." What God does for one, He is ready and willing to do for all. There are so many promises in the Word of God to meet each and every need—healing, finance, peace, or whatever the necessity.

Knowing God doesn't have favorites, let's take a look at what God's Word says about miracle accounts of widows in the Word. Get ready to be blessed and be a blessing! I know you are going to find yourself in one or more of these women. You will see the favor and mercy of God. "For You, Lord, will bless the [uncompromisingly] righteous [him who is in right standing with you]; as with a shield You will surround him with goodwill (pleasure and favor)" (Psalm 5:12 AMP). We can see from this Scripture that God surrounds us with goodwill, pleasure, and favor. And of course, He will do it!

Another wonderful Scripture to pray as we enter this study is Ephesians 1:17-19:

> That...the Father of glory, may give unto you the spirit of wisdom and revelation in the knowledge of Him, the eyes of your understanding being enlightened; that you may know what is the hope of His calling, and what are the riches of the glory of His inheritance in the saints, and what is the exceeding greatness of His power toward us who believe, according to the working of His mighty power. (NKJV)

Immediately you see God has an amazing plan for you. He had you in mind at the very foundation of the earth according to Ephesians 3. Hope is not lost for you. As long as you are alive, there is always time for a new beginning.

CHAPTER 3

Heaven's Provisions

In my research of the biblical accounts of widows, the Holy Spirit revealed five recurring themes, provisions, or benefits found throughout the Word of God: miracle provision, divine appointments, blessings on fatherless children, restoration in widows' lives, and new direction and destiny. There certainly may be more provisions for widows in the Word but these are the ones the Lord revealed to me. Again, we have already shared the Father heart of God is full of compassion toward widows and He desires to meet their needs as only God can. In future chapters we will review the lives of widows both in Old and New Testaments, and we will note each of these various themes. Remember as you read God doesn't play favorites! If He did it for one, He's obligated Himself to do it for you—if you will follow His instructions.

Miracle Provision

In many parts of the world—in Bible days as well as the 21st Century—women and especially widows were left to their own resources to care for themselves after the loss of their husband. Then and now, widows may lose a home, family, ability to provide food and clothing—the basic necessities of life. The foremost need to be activated oftentimes is that of miracle provisions. In many cases in the Scriptures we see these miracle provisions were certainly super-naturally meeting the widow's and her family's needs but on some occasions it was life-sustaining provision.

There have been numerous times when I had need of material items and God provided. I have seen the hand of God over and over and over. My church, World Outreach Church in Tulsa, Oklahoma, has missions in many parts of the world, as well as a Bible school called DOMATA School of Ministry. God opened a door for me to attend this Bible school about a year following the decease of my husband. Even the calling I received from God to go to DOMOTA was supernatural. It seems like my life has taken on a supernatural process from material goods, to divine appointments, to a new destiny. Once God spoke to me to attend Bible school, I only had a couple of days to get ready to go. I did not have anything that I needed and I only had about 48 hours to get ready. But God miraculously provided *everything*—from tuition, books, clothes, and so much more. Because I had been ill the year after my husband passed away I had lost over 70 pounds and my wardrobe was very limited. Several weeks into class our instructor was teaching on faith one day and by the Spirit he said, "You don't need to worry about what you are going wear, God knows your size and style." Now I know it was a statement to the whole class but I took it as a personal message to me. I had peace God knew right where I was. He had heard my prayers and He was working it out. A short time later a lady in our church ask me what size clothing I wore and said she was getting rid of some things in her closet and invited me to come and see if there was anything I could use. Of course there was and I came home that day praising and thanking God with a whole new wardrobe "just my size and style." God is ready to meet our every need! In the next chapter, we'll see how God has done this for widow after widow in Scripture. Again, God has no favorites.

Divine Appointments

Perhaps you're asking, *What is a divine appointment?* A divine appointment is an arrangement or supernatural meeting only God can put together and it is always for your good. A divine appointment is different from a coincidence or circumstance. A circumstance or coincidence is not always for your good; it could be an arrangement set up by the devil to harm you. But you want those divine appointments—a set up by God, to minister for your good and for your needs.

Many of our biblical examples had divine appointments. It has been amazing in my life how many divine appointments God has brought my way since my husband passed away. Only God can orchestrate these divine appointments. He did for me—He'll do it for you! Putting this book together involved one divine appointment after another. I did not know the first thing about the process and called a friend to pray with me about how to proceed. About an hour later she called me with the name of someone she thought might be able to help and the rest is history, as they say. Each time I needed to take the next step the next person would be available with their time and talent.

It is so marvelous how I have seen the hand of the Lord move in such miraculous ways. Even the writing of this book is one divine appointment and miracle after another. But as a new widow, I desperately needed fellowship. I wanted some mature women of faith who could encourage me in the Lord. I prayed or petitioned the Lord to send me some mature Christian women friends who would encourage me in my faith and walk with Him. God is not about just barely meeting your needs; He abounds in everything. "To Him Who is able to do exceedingly abundantly above all that we ask or think, according to the power that works in us, to Him *be* glory in the church by Christ Jesus" (Eph. 3:20-21 NKJV). God provided for me in abundance with wonderful Christian women of faith. These women are strong in the Word and prayer—women who enjoy talking about the Lord and His goodness, who are sensitive to the Holy Spirit, and find great joy in ministering to others. These women have provided me with wonderful examples of God's grace and mercy and I have grown much in getting to know them.

There are so many places in the Scriptures where God tells us just to ask Him to supply our needs—spirit, soul, and body. But we are told to do it in faith. Remember when we address God, we always pray to the Father in Jesus' name and we must always ask in faith—believing. "Without faith it is impossible to please Him" (Heb. 11:6). In Matthew 21:22 Jesus says, "And all things, whatsoever ye shall ask in prayer, believing, ye shall receive." As long as your request lines up with the Word and character of God, the promise from Jesus is that God your Father will do it for you.

Other divine appointments have occurred when the door seemed to be closed to make an appointment at a doctor or some other event, and God would turn the closed door into an open door. Sounds simple! But God is so ready to move into our life and perform impossible things when we believe and ask Him to do so.

Blessings on Fatherless Children

Just as God mentions widows in numerous places in the Bible and His provision for them, often you will see the Scriptures mentioning widows and the fatherless in one breath. An excellent Scripture is Psalm 68:5, "A father of the fatherless and a judge and protector of the widows is God in His holy habitation" (AMP). Through this Scripture and a myriad of others you see God has made provision for fatherless children. Tiny children are mentioned and even babies in Scripture receive God's special care. My children were adults— middle-aged adults—when I was widowed and yet I experienced God being a father to them who were fatherless as adults. I have seen God perform, work, and minister in their lives in powerful ways.

One huge obstacle God helped me to overcome regarding my children was to deliver me from that "feeling" it was my responsibility to take care of all of them. I was struggling to take care of myself, much less them. It was a great day of restoration when I realized I didn't have to be their answer. In fact, God orchestrated a situation where He wanted to deal with them. Having the courage to let go in the natural of your children is huge! But as I stood on the Word of God I saw God's deliverance in their lives. And the liberty that came to me when I saw God could and would take care of them was awesome!

Restoration in Widows' Lives

In Joel 2:25 the Amplified version reads, "And I will restore or replace for you the years that the locust have eaten." What a promise of God! That promise is one of those I have personalized and I pray it faithfully over myself and my home. In fact, I have prepared what I call a Prayer Bible that is chock-full of Post-It Notes, so I can easily pray Scriptures over my family, friends, church, nation, and myself. For example, I love to personalize and pray Ephesians 1:17-18 from The Amplified Bible:

> I pray that the God of our Lord Jesus Christ will grant me a spirit of wisdom and revelation of insight into mysteries and secrets in the deep intimate knowledge of Him, by having the eyes of my heart flooded with light, so I can know and understand the hope to which He has called me to and how rich is His glorious inheritance in the saints—His set apart ones.

Two other powerful Scriptures for peace and safety are Psalms 4:8 and Proverbs 3:24. I personalize these from The Amplified Bible as well:

> In peace I will both lie down and sleep, for you Lord alone make me dwell in safety and confident trust. When I lie down I shall not be afraid and my sleep shall be sweet. Thank You for these blessings in the name of Jesus.

I also pray Isaiah 54:13 over my children and grandchildren:

> I pray that all my children and grandchildren will be disciples taught of the Lord and obedient to His will and great shall be

the peace of my children and grandchildren, in the name of the Lord Jesus Christ.

God has wrought many divine restorations in me, but the primary one was a new door of ministry once again. Due to my husband's long illness, for many years I was his caretaker and we had to back off of certain privileges of those who are not fighting a terminal illness—going out to dinner, shopping, and taking short car trips which we both loved.

In my case and perhaps in yours, restoration and new destiny may blend together. They are often closely tied with each other. When God called me initially to go to Bible school, it dawned on my heart in that very moment that God would use me in some fashion to go to the world. At the time I did not know all God was doing. But it was the beginning of restoration of ministry and service in the Kingdom of God. This book is part of the beginning of new direction and His plans for me.

New Direction and Destiny

In Proverbs 29:18, we read, "Where there is no vision, the people perish...." I believe God has vision and direction for every widow. It is important to seek God to find that new direction or purpose for your life. Another favorite promise I stand on for a bright future is found in Jeremiah 29:11, "For I know the thoughts and plans that I have for you, says the Lord, thoughts and plans for welfare and peace and not for evil, to give you hope in your final outcome" (AMP).

My obedience to God was vital to me when I was struggling through those first few weeks and months of grief. How was I to know that very obedience to seek God in the midst of trouble would lead me into a new direction and destiny? Who would have ever known that seeking the Word of God for myself in my moment of trouble would not only be an answer to my immediate crisis but open up ministry to others?

What God does for you, He will do through you. The truth is God is purposeful! All of the blessings, gifts, and talents of God are for you, and they are also given to you so you can bless others.

My course was reset as God called me to go to Bible school. It revealed my calling to minister to widows with the healing power of God found in the Scriptures. I have not fully realized the breadth, depth, height, and width of where that vision will take me, but I took the first step of obedience to God—to seek Him and find what the Word of God said about setting widows free who were caught in the mire of depression and hopelessness. And further obedience has come by writing what God has given me, for all who will avail themselves to it. God is truly a "whosoever God." Let God redirect your course and give you the future He has planned just for you.

CHAPTER 4

Biblical Examples

Let's take a look at some biblical examples of widows who were blessed, restored, provided for, and set on a new course God destined for them. Keep in mind that just as God brings fulfillment, safety, and miracle provision to so many in the Word of God, He will also do it for you. He's the same God today as He always has been.

Widow of Zarephath

A favorite account of mine is from 1 Kings 17. King Ahab and his wife, Jezebel, are rulers over Israel, and they are bent on killing Elijah because of his prophecy against Israel. The Spirit of God spoke judgment upon Israel through Elijah because King Ahab and Jezebel set up an idol to worship. According to Elijah, there would be no rain or even dew for three-and-a-half years.

During this time the Lord protects Elijah and hides him. God sends him to the Brook Cherith and ravens feed him there. Once the brook runs dry God prophesies that a widow in Zarephath will sustain him.

In Scripture this widow is unnamed. She is an idol worshiper, and she does not know Elijah's God. Elijah "happens" to meet her outside of the city where the well is located—another divine appointment foretold by God.

In that day and time, it was polite or hospitable to get water for a stranger or whoever might ask you. Elijah sees the widow and he asks her to get him some water. As she goes to get Elijah water he says, "Please bring me a morsel of bread in your hand" (v. 11 NKJV).

The widow responds, "As the Lord *your* God lives..." (v. 12 NKJV, italics mine). To me this is a critical statement. She knows that "his" God is a living God. It's been over two years now that they've had no rain and no dew. There is famine in the land. But she separates "her god" from "his God." She continues, "I do not have bread, only a handful of flour in a bin, and a little oil in a jar; and see, I *am* gathering a couple of sticks that I may go in and prepare it for myself and my son, that we may eat it, and die" (v. 12 NKJV).

When Elijah tells her that if she will make him a cake first, the flour will never run dry, nor will the oil, she responds by doing all that Elijah asks. She makes him a little cake and brings him the water. We know from the Scriptures God supplies all of their food, water, and oil until the rain finally comes. However, during that time her child becomes sick and dies and Elijah raises him from the dead! Not only did God meet her material provision miraculously, He also met her physical, emotional, and relationship needs by raising her child from the dead. We see healing for her child and blessing on her household.

This is certainly an example of restoration as the widow gets her son back *and* she gets her own life back! They would have both be dead without the miracles. The widow becomes a believer! We see this change of heart in 1 Kings 17:24: "And the woman said to Elijah, Now by this I know that thou art a man of God, and that the word of the Lord in thy mouth is truth."

Prophet's Widow

The widow of 2 Kings 4 finds deliverance through the hand of the prophet Elisha, who is Elijah's successor. I call her the prophet's widow because she was married to a prophet. She is another unnamed widow in Scripture, but is the center of a very popular story nonetheless.

With her husband gone, the widow is left with unpaid bills and debts. The creditors threaten to come and take her children away as collateral for the debt. In that day creditors could make slaves out of children in order to pay off a family's debt. To lose your husband and then your children would be completely overwhelming.

When the widow cries out to Elisha, he asks her, "What do you have in the house?" (v. 2, NKJV). All she has is a little bit of oil but Elisha blesses the oil. He tells her to go out and get as many containers as she can from her neighbors. She instructs her sons to go out and do as the prophet said locating as many pots as possible. Once she has the containers she begins to fill them and finds the oil keeps pouring out of her little jar until every container is full. She then sells the oil and earns enough money to pay all of her debts. It's a case of miraculous provision and her children are no longer obligated to be slaves.

Another widow receives a provisional miracle; her debts are removed and her children are safe. Amazingly, another destiny changes!

Shunammite Woman

The Shunammite in 2 Kings 4:8 is a barren woman married to a wealthy, older man. Elisha passes her way often and the couple builds a chamber for him. Due to this woman's kindness to Elisha, he blesses her and tells her she will have a son. All of this is because of her kindness to minister to Elisha's needs.

The child is born and at about 12-years-old the boy is working out in the field with his father when he has a fatal heatstroke. Elisha hears the news and comes to the home. Then he raises the boy from the dead—another miraculous event. It would seem this woman has one miracle after another—certainly, a believer in an El Shaddai God.

In 2 Kings 8:1, Elisha warns the Shunammite woman of a famine the Lord is calling on the land. She and her son go away per Elisha's warning and we assume her husband has died. The widow is away from her home for several years, but then returns.

The Shunammite woman went to the king to make an appeal to return ownership of her house and her land. The Bible records that Gehazi, Elisha's servant is also present. The king asks Gehazi to recount some of the miraculous things in Elisha's ministry. As Gehazi starts to tell about the Shunammite woman's son and how Elisha raised him from the dead, Gehazi points out the widow and appeals for her house and land. Talk about divine appointment. Normally, kings would retain the land because that's how they gained property when people left the country during a famine.

This Shunammite woman once again is blessed! She gets her land back and her child has a heritage. The king also restores all that was hers including the money she would have earned had she been living on the land while she was gone. This is a truly blessed woman!

Widow at Nain

We now turn to the New Testament and find Jesus as the Deliverer for a widow in Luke, chapter 7. Jesus was traveling with his disciples to a city called Nain and a large crowd was with them. As they near the gate, they see a funeral procession coming down the road; the young man was the only son of his mother, a widow from Nain.

The Bible calls this son a "young man" contrary to some traditional Sunday school materials referencing him as a child. The key here is to know that it is her only son. Without a husband and now her only son dying, the widow was losing her only source of material provision. They didn't have Medicare and Social Security. His death meant she was without income and most likely a place to live.

Jesus comes on the scene—again at the moment of her need, another divine appointment. The Scriptures say Jesus had compassion on the widow and raised the boy from the dead. The blessing of her son being raised up is certainly a restoration of her son's life, but it is also a miracle provision. She would have been homeless and without income or help if this miracle had not sustained her son's life. Her life and destiny is turned around by this one act of Jesus!

Dorcas

In chapter 9 of the Acts of the Apostles, we see Dorcas, an invaluable Christian worker for God. The Bible boasts her to be a woman who abounded in good deeds and acts of charity to widows. We are told she is a seamstress and a friend to widows, but we are unsure if she is a widow. In those days, Dorcas became sick and died. The widows in the Church of Joppa were distraught at the loss of Dorcas, and they didn't know what they were going to do without her. The disciples there heard Peter was in a nearby town, so they sent for him. When Peter came they brought him to the upper room where Dorcas was laid. He prayed and she opened her eyes and sat up! Peter presented her alive to the saints and widows.

Tamar

Being in the lineage of Jesus always gives people significance in the Old Testament. This is Tamar's life purpose or assignment from God. Genesis 38 tells her story and the trauma accompanying her life including being widowed twice. From our cultural perspective, her deed is an outrageous thing to do.

In that time, if a woman's husband died, she would be given to the next brother to raise up a seed (a child) to receive the inheritance the deceased husband would have received. In Tamar's case, her husband dies and she is given to her husband's brother, who also dies. Her Father-in-law, Judah, promises Tamar she would become the wife of the third son when he came of age. But out of fear that something would happen to this son also, Judah does not give Tamar to him as wife when he comes of age.

In short, Tamar deceptively poses as a prostitute and she has intimacy with Judah, the son of Jacob (Israel), who brings forth her destiny, even though he ignored, dispelled, and rejected her. Again, women were at the bottom of the rung and second-class citizens in her day. She basically takes her life and destiny into her own hands. If you look at what happens, she is justified by God. She is a determined and courageous woman and she is destined to fulfill her life purpose. She gives birth to twins from Judah—children she is ordained to have by God. So Tamar receives "blessings on her children." God restores her life by returning her back to the very plan of God for her life in the first place. Her destiny continues. She accomplishes what she is destined to do!

Abigail

In 1 Samuel 25 Abigail is married to a very wealthy but evil man, Nabal. David and his 600 men are hiding in caves running from King Saul. They had protected Nabal's sheep for he and his men to eat, but now Nabal will not help David when he asks. David decides to kill Nabal's men. Nabal has more than enough to share, but refuses. Nabal is evil and greedy—probably influenced by Satan to stop David! Abigail sees what is happening and has her servants gather food to feed the 600 men. She goes out to meet David and provides for his men's needs. She falls down on her face and apologizes on behalf of her husband. She says, "On me let this iniquity be" (v. 24, NKJV). What is interesting is David thanks her because "she" kept him from blood-guiltiness. In other words, Abigail knows David will someday be the king, and he will not have anything to regret. He will know God took care of him in the past and he didn't have to defend himself. Abigail goes home and sees her husband who is drunk. Waiting until the next morning, she finally tells him what she did. Nabal has a stroke or seizure of some kind within ten days and dies.

Abigail is now a widow, thus included in this chapter. Eventually, she marries David. Abigail as a widow did not need material provision, but God replaces and restores an evil husband with a kind and God fearing husband. It changes her destiny!

Bathsheba

We see the story of Bathsheba unfold in 2 Samuel 11. She is not a widow when we first see her but is married to a soldier in David's army. David observes her bathing and sends some of his men to bring her to him. Hollywood depicts the account of David and Bathsheba as a love affair. Of course, Bathsheba could not say *no* to the king. She has to go when the king calls for her. I am not sure if I would have loved David if he had killed my husband.

We know Bathsheba becomes pregnant and she and King David lose the child because of God's judgment on David's sin including disobedience to God's instructions. Bathsheba has a total of four children by King David. The second one is Solomon, who becomes king after David. We see him listed in the lineage of Joseph, Jesus' step-father, in Matthew 1:6. Bathsheba's third son is Nathan. By reviewing the genealogy in Luke 3:31, which is Mary's genealogy (Jesus' mother), we find she came down through the line of Nathan.

Bathsheba experiences restoration through remarriage and the three children born after the one she lost. What a heritage belongs to her despite the calamity and trauma of her life. Her destiny changes!

Summary

In how many of these accounts did we see miracle provision, either with food, a home, or a husband? Many of these widows had supernatural divine appointments. We see great blessings on children of widows. We also see restoration in some area of their lives, or a new destiny or direction.

These women represent all types of widows: young and old, rich and poor; some with children; others with no children; some were believers in God; others were not in the beginning. God wants us to see He can and will care for all types of widows, no matter what has happened in one's life. These biblical accounts were given to us as examples of God's provision as we see from 1 Corinthians 10:11: "Now these things befell them by way of a figure [as an example and warning to us]; they were written to admonish and fit us for right action by good instruction, we in whose days the ages have reached their climax (their consummation and concluding period)" (AMP).

Three of the widows mentioned in this book—Tamar, Ruth, and Bathsheba—all appear in the list of descendants of Jesus in the first chapter of Matthew. You'll find more to Ruth's story in chapter 6, but first we'll look at the promises God has for widows.

CHAPTER 5

Heaven's Promises

As you've already seen, answers from God's perspective to a widow's struggles are found in the Word of God. In this chapter we are going to delineate promises specifically to widows as well as general promises in God's Word that are applicable in widow's lives. You can personalize and pray these Scriptures over your own life and situations and see divine results.

You've perhaps heard the phrase "claim the promises." What does that mean? Truly in many Christians' lives there is a time where the Bible comes alive and it becomes more than just a U.S. Library of Congress book. It becomes "The Book" a Christian wants to live by. My story of how the Bible came alive and became a living and breathing part of my daily life, may encourage you to dig deeper into the Scriptures.

God and His Word dramatically changed my life when I was 32-years-old. I had been in church my whole life, and I loved going to church. But I did not have a personal relationship with the Lord until I asked Jesus to come into my life as Savior and Lord at age 32.

Becoming a new creation in Christ through receiving Jesus Christ into my heart and life changed everything for me. We learn from 2 Corinthians 5:17, "Therefore if any man be in Christ, he is a new creature: old things are passed away; behold, all things are become new." Every believer in Christ has two births: a natural birth when he is born into the earth through his mother's womb and a spiritual birth when he receives Christ. To receive eternal life you must experience both a natural and a spiritual birth (John 3).

When you are born of God, you receive the nature of God. Second Peter 1:4 says you become a partaker of God's nature. This change, of course, takes place in your spirit. Your physical body does not change. If you had brown hair and blue eyes before salvation, you will still have brown hair and blue eyes after you are born again. Your body and soul do not change, only your spirit.

The Living Word of God

When I became a believer in Jesus Christ in 1973, the Word of God came alive to me. It was so exciting to me! Five days later I received the baptism of the Holy Spirit. God poured His love through me. I never knew anything like that existed. It was amazing—the love that God poured into me. It was one of those "aha" moments. My whole life changed!

With the new birth experience, I had a love for God and for people that radiated and excelled anything I had ever experienced. As a result of this spiritual regeneration, the Bible took on a whole new understanding. Prior to this I read my Bible, but I didn't understand it. With this new light, I began to see God was speaking to me—His will, His plan, and all of the inheritance He had provided for me through Jesus Christ from the Word. Now as I read the Bible, I see the promises of God that He planned from the beginning.

In the Gospel of John, chapter 15, verse 7, it reads, "If ye abide in me, and my words abide in you, ye shall ask what ye will, and it shall be done unto you." In order to access the promises of God and receive the answers and blessings God has provided, you have to know what God has promised you.

The Word of God is full of power. In Hebrews 4:12 the Bible says, "For the Word of God is quick, and powerful, and sharper than any twoedged sword, piercing even to the dividing asunder of soul and spirit, and of the joints and marrow, and is a discerner of the thoughts and intents of the heart." In short, that verse simply means that the Word of God will minister not just to your heart or spirit, but to your body and soul—mind, will, and emotions. God has given us power to minister to every aspect of our life and these answers for all of life's issues are coming to us from God's Word. We must read God's promises, think on them, and confess them (or pray them). Then according to John 15:7, God will bring His Words that we embrace, access, and speak out of our mouth to pass.

God's Promises

A promise is simply a word of guarantee or declaration someone will do something or give you something. The Bible says God is not a liar (Num. 23:19); and He will uphold His Word to a thousand generations (Deut. 7:9). In Jeremiah 1:12, it says, "I will hasten my word to perform it."

All you and I as believers have to do is to find God's Word and put His Word in our mouth through confession or prayer, and believe God will bring it to pass on our behalf.

Let's begin to look at some of the promises God has made to us as widows in the Word of God. We've already seen how God, over and over again, brought supernatural miracles of provision, healing, deliverance, favor, and brand new lives with purpose and meaning to widows in the Bible. Hebrews 13:8 says, "Jesus Christ, the same yesterday, and today, and forever." What He did for one, He's obligated Himself to do for all who call upon Him.

God Provides Material Needs

In many cases widows are in need of basic provision such as food, clothing, and other material needs. Below are Bible promises to personalize and pray over your needs.

For the Lord your God is God of gods and Lord of lords, the great, the mighty...God, Who is not partial and takes no bribe. He executes justice for the fatherless and the widow... and gives him food and water. (Deut. 10:17-18, AMP)

God is able to take care of us. He is able to feed us and cloth us in a mighty way. He has done it for me over and over again. He is able to bless us in ways we can't imagine and He executes justice for us.

Now remember God is a good God! He has made provision for us as widows way before we were in this situation. Sometimes as people in a carnal (flesh-ruled), natural state, we may have tried to manipulate people to get a need met. But our relationship with God is totally different. We may think for God to answer our prayers or meet our needs we have to con or manipulate God because we are not "good enough." But we don't have to be good enough in the natural for God to use His power to do something for us. We are already good enough in Christ. We have been made righteous in Christ Jesus (1 Cor. 1:30). If you are in Christ, then it is God's will to take care of His children. Because of incorrect teaching in the Church, we may have thought we had to earn God's righteousness to receive His blessings. But that would be to dishonor the sacrifice Christ made for us to be in right standing with God.

Perhaps our thinking is if I just pray enough or read the Bible enough, or serve God in the church, then God will help me. Well, guess what? God will not be bribed by our religious deeds. Church attendance, reading our Bible, praying long hours, and fasting for days does not change His mind. We do these things because we love God. He is only looking at our hearts.

And my God will liberally supply (fill to the full) your every need according to His riches in glory. (Phil. 4:19, AMP)

God promises to supply our needs, not according to any of our resources, but according to His riches in glory. His supply is abundant!

God, my Shepherd! I don't need a thing. You have bedded me down in lush meadows, you find me quiet pools to drink from. True to your word, you let me catch my breath and send me in the right direction. Even when the way goes through Death Valley, I'm not afraid when you walk at my side. Your trusty shepherd's crook makes me feel secure. You serve me a six-course dinner right in front of my enemies. You revive my drooping head; my cup brims with blessing. Your beauty and love chase after me every day of my life. I'm back home in the house of God for the rest of my life. (Psalm 23, MSG)

Again, we see God providing not only material needs, such as a home and food, but security, rest, and help in the midst of trouble. What a mighty God we serve! He is reliable in the midst of our midnight hour and storm. He will rescue and provide for our every need.

Religious worship (true worship)…in the sight of God the Father is this: to visit and help and care for the orphans and widows in their affliction and need. (James 1:27, AMP, parentheses mine)

Again, God's intent is to cause those who are in the Church to be agents of blessing and welfare to widows and their children who are in need. This is another strong promise of help from our Heavenly Father.

God Provides Favor and Blessing

For You, Lord, will bless the [uncompromisingly] righteous [him who is upright and in right standing with You]; as with a shield You will surround him with goodwill (pleasure and favor). (Psalm 5:12, AMP)

And Jesus increased in wisdom and stature, and in favor with God and man. (Luke 2:52)

Favor with God and man belongs to the son and daughter of God. Pray for favor. It belongs to you as a daughter of God. There may be times when an appointment is needed but no openings seem to be available, but the favor of God will result in a phone call announcing, "There is a cancellation!" As I've prayed and asked God for favor I've seen this happen over and over. So many supernatural things have happened. Favor is yours for the asking and don't get upset over delays. God can turn them around for your good.

> The Lord shall command the blessing upon you in your storehouse and in all that you undertake. And He will bless you in the land which the Lord your God gives you. (Deuteronomy 28:8, AMP)

The 28th chapter of Deuteronomy lists the blessings (and the curses) of those who hearken or give heed to the voice of the Lord and obey His Word. But truly God is desiring His kids lack for nothing and have their needs abundantly supplied—spirit, soul, and body.

God is a Companion/Helper

> And let [those who have been made] your widows trust and confide in me. (Jer. 49:11, AMP)

A great challenge when your husband dies is having someone with whom to talk. Guess Who is there? God is our confidante. He is there 24/7 no matter where you are or what the situation; you can confide in God, your Heavenly Father, as your counsel.

> Fear not, for you shall not be ashamed; neither be confounded and depressed, for you shall not be put to shame. For you shall forget the shame of your youth, and you shall not

[seriously] remember the reproach of your widowhood any more. For your Maker is your Husband—the Lord of Hosts is His name—the Holy One of Israel is your Redeemer; the God of the whole earth He is called. (Isaiah 54:4-5, AMP)

This Scripture is not just for widows, but certainly is applicable. Our Maker is our Husband. He takes that place as Provider, as One Who loves us. As believers we must spend time worshiping Him and fellowshipping with Him daily. By talking to Him daily He fills us up with Himself and meets even our soul needs for fellowship in a way that no one else can!

For He [God] Himself has said, I will not in any way fail you nor give you up nor leave you without support. [I will] not, [I will] not, [I will] not in any degree leave you helpless nor forsake nor let [you] down (relax My hold on you)! [Assuredly not!] So we take comfort and are encouraged and confidently and boldly say, The Lord is My Helper; I will not be seized with alarm [I will not fear or dread or be terrified]. What can man do to me? (Hebrews 13:5-6, AMP)

We have a Helper in our God—He truly is our Helper! He is with us through all the difficult decisions. He is with us through everything we have to do each and every day. With the Lord as our Companion and our Helper, and as we put our trust in His ability to do what no man can do, fear and terror have no place in us.

God Brings Peace and Sleep

In peace I will both lie down and sleep, for You, Lord, alone make me dwell in safety and confident trust. (Psalm 4:8, AMP)

I had never lived alone until my husband was placed in a nursing home. At first it was uncomfortable—a very different experience, for sure. It was amazing to actually have the TV remote to myself—totally awesome! But the new small luxuries did not in any way compensate for not having the person I loved by my side.

Probably one of the greatest challenges in living alone was going to sleep without my husband. This Scripture was a great comfort to me and helped me get rest and sleep. The words "I will" are the strongest proclamations in the English language. It's a declaration! I *will* lie down and sleep! Why? For the Lord alone *makes* me dwell safely!

Casting the whole of your care [all your anxieties, all your worries, all your concerns, once and for all] on Him, for He cares for you affectionately and cares about you watchfully. (1 Peter 5:7, AMP)

This is one of the most difficult but stress-relieving Scriptures in the Bible in which to be a doer. We are told to cast *all* our cares over on Him. He designed us so that we would never have to worry. Can you believe that? He doesn't want us to worry about anything. This will lead to a more peaceful life.

God is Healer—Body and Soul

Surely He has borne our griefs (sicknesses, weaknesses, and distresses) and carried our sorrows and pains [of punishment]...But He was wounded for our transgressions, he was bruised for our guilt and iniquities; the chastisement needful to obtain peace and well-being for us was upon Him and with the stripes [that wounded] Him we are healed and made whole. (Isaiah 53:4-5, AMP)

One of the greatest challenges of widowhood obviously is the grief and emotional upheaval that comes at the loss of a spouse. There are times of grief, distress, or feelings of sorrow that at times paralyze and overtake you. Thanks to the Lord's great plan, Jesus experienced not only the penalty for our sin, but He also paid for our emotional freedom by bearing in Himself our bitterness, hurt, and sorrow; we have been freed. Because Jesus knew of His coming separation from His Father at the cross, He experienced such overwhelming sorrow that He produced great drops of blood in the Garden of Gethsemane while He was praying and consecrating Himself anew to His Father. None of us have ever experienced sorrow to that extent in this life. Know that through Jesus, God has made a way for us in our darkest hour. He wants to bring His soul salvation to us with His divine peace in the midst of the upheaval.

...and with His stripes that wounded Him we are healed and made whole. (Isaiah 53:5, AMP)

He bore on His back 39 stripes which represents all of the major diseases in the world, so you and I could walk free. The wholeness

He bought is physical (for our body) *and* mental (for our soul). The Hebrew words "Jehovah Shalom" mean *nothing missing and nothing broken.*[2] He suffered at the cross for you and I to walk free of pain—both physical and mental.

God is Your Protector

You shall not afflict any widow or fatherless child. If you afflict them in any way and they cry at all to me, I will surely hear their cry. (Exodus 22:22-23, AMP)

The word "afflict" in *Strong's Exhaustive Concordance* means: "To look down upon, to depress, to deal harshly with, to defile, to hurt, to ravish, to exercise force against, or to weaken in any way."[3]

This is a vital promise of God declaring that as a widow if you're being afflicted in "any" way or being looked down upon, you can go to the Father and He will surely hear your cry.

We see in so many passages where God is definitely your protector. In the next verse we'll see that the Word of God inexplicably states it.

A father of the fatherless and a judge and protector of the widows is God in His holy habitation. (Psalm 68:5, AMP)

Thank God for His protection. You can't get a clearer statement of God preserving and protecting us as widows.

The Lord tears down the house of the proud, but He makes secure the boundaries of the [consecrated] widow. (Proverbs 15:25, AMP)

What a glorious promise of God! This is a favorite of mine. I pray and give God thanks daily for securing the boundaries of my home, all of my property, and all of my children and grandchildren, and their borders.

> The Lord protects and preserves the strangers and temporary residents, He upholds the fatherless and the widow and sets them upright. (Psalm 146:9, AMP)

God has our back; He is for us—certainly not against us. He has promised once again to protect, preserve, and uphold us. How wonderful is our Lord and God!

> There shall no evil befall you, nor any plague or calamity come near your tent. For He will give His angels [especial] charge over you to accompany and defend and preserve you in all your ways. (Psalm 91:10-11, AMP)

God's full intention is to protect and preserve those who call upon Him and are called by His Name.

We started out this chapter discussing God's promises to His children and especially to His widows and orphans. But as with every child of God His promises don't just occur because we're good-looking or have some special gifting. We receive God's promises as we acknowledge and confess them to Him, in belief and trust. We have a connection with God through our faith, which is released by our mouth. As you read the Scriptures out loud you hear God's personal promises to you, enabling your heart to believe and receive what belongs to you.

CHAPTER 6

Overcoming Hurt And Bitterness

"A Mandate Before Destiny Emerges"

We have discussed promise after promise God has given to the widow and orphans in the Word of God. We have talked about God providing for us materially and providing favor to us in circumstances. We have noted the protecting ability of God on our behalf. We have seen how God is with us and certainly for us. We have learned God is even concerned about our rest and sleep at night.

However, a great obstacle that many widows never seem to overcome is anger or bitterness either at their spouse, God, or someone else. Many times it is not clearly understood or perhaps not even identified as anger or bitterness. In order to move on with life and move into the new direction or destiny God has for us, we have to surmount this obstacle called hurt, bitterness, or anger.

I left the story of Naomi in the Book of Ruth for us to review in this chapter. Through Naomi's story we see how God aided her to overcome and find peace in herself and experience the future blessing of God.

The whole Book of Ruth has always been one of my favorite Bible accounts. However, I never realized how powerful and personal it was until I became a widow. We see Naomi and her husband left Israel to go to another country because of the famine in Bethlehem. To shorten a long story, her husband passed away as well as both of her sons who were married. Basically, Naomi and her two daughters-in-law were very poor. Naomi decided she was returning home to Bethlehem because she heard things were better back home. She told the girls to go back to their father's homes. They both cried and told Naomi, "Surely we will return with you to your people." However, Orpah finally decided to go back to her parents, and we never hear from her again. Ruth went with Naomi and proclaimed the popular Scripture that is used in many weddings, "For wherever you go I will go; and wherever you lodge, I will lodge; your people shall be my people, and your God my God." It refers to two widows, Ruth and Naomi, a daughter-in-law and her mother-in-law.

On the way back home, Naomi expressed her bitterness. *How can this happen to me? Poor me!* Self-pity is a common stage many widows experience. The questions posed by many widows is the same as what Noami expressed: *Why me?*

I, too, fell into the same trap as Naomi. My husband and I had plans for our retirement years and we had ministry plans for the future. I remember sitting at his bedside when he was gone thinking, "*What am I going to do for the rest of my life? What am I going to do?*

Everything I have is wrapped up in him and what we would do together. And here I am alone."

I was under tremendous pressure, grief, and sorrow. I couldn't seem to shake it for quite a period of time. As you will see in a later chapter, God took care of it miraculously when I was *doing* what He called me to do.

Healing from Bitterness

On New Year's Day 2007, my husband said he was going to leave (for Heaven). He didn't die until he said he was ready to go. Nine years earlier we were told by doctors that he could go any day. For nine years we lived together with the uncertainty of wondering if today was his last day. When Fred reported that he was going to go to Heaven, I thought I had already dealt with hurt and bitterness since we experienced such a long illness. However, I did get mad—not at God—but at my husband because he just gave up one day. Once he proclaimed he was leaving, within 34 days he was gone.

A few days before Fred moved to Heaven we knew he would be going soon and I wanted to be with him when he went. I did not ask for what happened next but I want to share it with you now because it was such a blessing to me, and many of you have had similar experiences. We are never to ask for these experiences, but if they come we can thank God for them because they will always bring us peace.

As I was sitting there, holding Fred's hand, I began to see a spiritual veil between heaven and earth. I had heard people talk about the veil, but never experienced it. My mother, my father, and the child my husband and I lost were standing on the other side of this veil. I could see them clearly. It would be as if there were a very thick veil or sheer and they were standing just on the other side. I knew who they were and that was such a comfort to me. I said to the Lord afterward, "Why were my parents on the other side of the veil when Fred's parents are both in heaven, too?" The Lord told me, "It was to comfort you." We had a child who was lost before he was born, but he wasn't a baby anymore. He was a half-grown child.

For the next few days, I could still see them. It was such a comfort. In fact, it was so real. I thought if I could reach through that veil, I could feel them. I even tried to reach through the veil but I couldn't.

The instant my husband was gone, they were gone too. Instantly they were all gone! It was such a blessing to me to know that when he went, there were loved ones waiting to greet him. Praise God! I believe it's supposed to be that way. Now, I know they'll be there to greet me if the rapture doesn't come first.

The Blessing of the Lord

Let's go back to where we left Naomi and Ruth. Naomi was bitter. And precious Ruth, she had lost her husband, too, but she just took care of Naomi and continued the journey. When they arrived at Naomi's home of Bethlehem they experienced a variety of divine appointments. Ruth was in the right field at the right time with the right person, eating the right food with the right group of people. You have to read the entire Book of Ruth to see all of the divine appointments they had. When Naomi finds out Ruth was in the field of one of her husband's relatives, Boaz, she said, *Look! He's our kinsman redeemer! He can redeem us! He can redeem the land! Everything we lost he can redeem it all!* Ruth is so obedient. She does whatever Naomi tells her to do.

When Boaz goes to the city gates the next day to check to see if another kinsman is a closer relative to Ruth than himself, the right person just happens to be there—another divine appointment! Boaz was given the right of redemption. He redeemed Naomi and Ruth and He became Ruth's husband. The women were restored and given a home. Ruth received a husband. The Bible says Boaz was a wealthy man, so Ruth's and Naomi's living arrangements were much better than they had before. Isn't that just like God? "The blessing of the Lord, it maketh rich, and he addeth no sorrow with it" (Prov. 10:22).

Ruth has a child of promise since Boaz is also in the lineage of Jesus. If you look in the Book of Matthew, Ruth is also named in the lineage of Jesus. Her little son becomes the grandfather of King David. In Ruth's case, we see provisional miracles and a new housing arrangement. We also see restoration because God replaced their whole lives with Ruth receiving a new husband, a new home, and a child of her own. How wonderful is that! And of course, Ruth's destiny was changed!

It is interesting when Naomi first appears in her home town, all the ladies are gossiping about her. *Oh, look at Naomi! Poor Naomi! She looks so discouraged and poor.* But after the little baby was born, they were all gathered around her, and she became the nurse to this little boy. This is one of the most amazing stories. God did so much for these widows and God is no respecter of persons (Acts 10:34).

Letting Go of Bitterness

Had Ruth not followed in the steps she did, the provision of God for Naomi would never have come to fruition. It was obviously in the plan of God that Ruth sensed a strong pull to Naomi. This was definitely a situation of her steps being directed of the Lord. But had Naomi kept up her resistance, bitterness, and self-pity, she could have blocked the full plan of God for both her and Ruth.

Notice the choice to "let go" of the hurt, anger, and bitterness had to come before the miracle provision, restoration, blessings, and destiny could come forth. Faith in action on what God has said is required before we see any supernatural manifestations of blessings in our lives.

Knowing Jesus bore our emotional pain and sorrow just like He did our physical pain must become a reality. We must release unforgiveness, hurt, and bitterness because those are Satan's tools. God cannot use the devil's ammunitions to bring His blessings to us. Those are simply tools God does not use.

We read in Ephesians 4:31, Paul's letter to the church in Ephesus, to let go of the root of bitterness, anger, and malice. Obviously, there was something going on in the church Paul had to address. You can let it go because Jesus bore the pain, hurt, and bitterness for you. If Jesus bore it already, you don't have to bear it. If you won't release that pain and grief to Jesus and you hold on to that hurt, you *stop* God's future for you. The blessings and plans He has for you are contingent upon you operating in His commandment of love and forgiveness.

But praise God, Naomi let go of the anger, hurt, and bitterness and trusted God to pull them through. If you are struggling in this area, take time now to ask God to help you release all bitterness and anger. In the next chapter you'll find the power of God's Word to help you to stay free.

CHAPTER 7

Victory In The Word

"Deliverance from Grief by God's Word"

As we've seen in the Word of God Jesus Himself bore our grief, hurt, and sorrow. But we have to take the Word of God for ourselves and receive His redemption, His healing of our hurts and sorrows. It's so vital for us to immerse ourselves in the Word of God regarding God's provision for our lives. It is in this immersion process or overdosing on the Word of God that redemption, healing, and victory comes.

In John 10:10 we read, "The thief comes only in order to steal and kill and destroy. I came that they may have and enjoy life, and have it in abundance (to the full, till it overflows)" (AMP). Those are the words of Jesus in the Gospel of John. It is the dividing line between the works of Jesus and the plans of God for His children, and the will of Satan. We can instantly know if something is not from God by this Bible verse. If it steals, kills, or destroys, it is from Satan your adversary. The Bible tells us we have authority against the works of the devil (Acts 10:38). When we see something that does not line up with God's plan for us, we need to use the Word of God and stand our ground against it.

During the loss of a husband, the drama, pain, and sorrow is great. However, if we have the Word of God in our armory either before, during, or after, we can fight the fight of faith that is required to go on to victory.

You may have heard it said a time or two "when it rains, it pours" referring to trouble. Of course, trouble only comes from Satan. God is a good God and He has promised us His blessings and life abundant. But this world and its system are run by the devil, so we have to decide to stand our ground on the Word of God if we are going to win our battles. Jesus has already won for us, but we *have to agree with Him*. If we allow our words, thoughts, and actions to be in harmony and in agreement with the devil, we'll fall for his schemes. If we don't take an offensive stand, we'll be one more Christian deceived and debilitated. Satan's plans go forward and God's will is thwarted.

To add further to the emotional duress and grief, if we continue in it by yielding to depression and oppression, a wide door can be opened for the devil to put sickness and disease in our lives. I have seen it occur in many widows' lives. The words of "I don't care if I live anymore" are heard redounding.

God gave to Adam or the first man the power to control his destiny. He gave man free will. However, the enemy would like to control man's free will just like he did with Adam in the Garden of Eden.

The Blessing of Obedience

I also know by firsthand experience what yielding to continual depression does as it did to me on the wings of my husband's death. I had been widowed only a few short months when I became weak and had great difficulty breathing. Doctors soon discovered blood clots in both of my lungs.

I was admitted to the hospital four times that summer. It was a serious situation. As a result of this infirmity in my body I couldn't allow myself to even grieve for my husband. If I cried I couldn't breathe. It was such a difficult time in my life. However, to God be the glory, I had already found all of those Scriptures about what God would do and provide for widows. I knew the Word and I had placed it in my heart in abundance. I meditated on the restoration and blessing Scriptures God had provided for widows as I had studied the Bible. Somehow I knew God was going to take care of me. Obviously, in this process I was ready to join my husband in Heaven. However, God's plans were higher than my plans!

One of the most important things in widowhood is to find purpose and destiny in life. Without it, it is easy to give in and quit life.

During this time of being very sick, my grandchildren were ages ten, nine, eight, and four. My daughter-in-law called me after attending church on a Wednesday night letting me know they were all coming over to pray for me. The grandchildren trooped into my house and stood by my chair. They put their little hands on me and began to pray. They prayed to the Father to heal me. At the time I was so sick I didn't think I would make it. My second oldest grandson understood in his childlike faith John 10:10, which says Jesus came to give us life and life more abundant; but the devil comes to steal, kill, and destroy. They lost their grandpa and they were going to do everything they knew to do to not lose their grandma. So my little grandson prayed and took authority over the devil and he claimed my healing by faith. He cast out the devil saying, "Leave my grandma alone in Jesus' name!"

They were only there ten minutes and then they left. After they were gone I knew that I knew that I knew I had to fight for my life. I could not let these grandchildren think God did not answer their prayers.

At this time I was advised I could not live alone. My son and his family invited me to stay with them, which I did. For the next ten months I fought for every breath.

Little did I know that the obedience to do what God told me—to find the Scriptures on widowhood in the Bible—would be my salvation. As I lay there sick in bed I would meditate on what the Scriptures said. When I was weak, I would remember the prayer of my grandchildren. In time, I improved and was able to eventually move into my own place. Those early months of seeking God's Word and immersing myself in the Bible were a doorway to God's purpose for me. However, little did I know it at the time.

A New Destiny

A year or so passed, and I had a divine appointment while attending church on a Sunday morning. I could have easily missed this divine appointment by not going to church that morning. God's appointments can happen almost anywhere while we are in the middle of living our daily lives.

This particular Sunday was Missions Sunday. (My church is a very missions-minded church.) Communion was also served that Sunday and we filed up to the front to received the communion elements from the pastor, and then returned to our chairs so we could all partake together.

After everyone has been served our pastor always asks if every-one has been served so that no one is left out. The Pastor proceeded to ask, "Is there anyone here who hasn't been served?" Missionaries started standing up dressed in native costumes from the nations they represented. Each one would tell how many in their nations had not yet been served with the Gospel of Christ yet.

At that moment God dropped in my heart the word "missions"—going to the world. If you can't go to the world, then send others, but do something! I looked over at a friend I was sitting with and said, "I think I am supposed to go to DOMATA." As I mentioned earlier, our church has a Bible school named DOMATA.

At the end of the service my friend introduced me to the assistant to the director of DOMATA. Less than two days later, I started Bible school. God met every need imaginable for me to attend in just a short span of time. Of course, I needed everything. I needed tuition, food, and clothes. And one-by-one-by-one everything I needed was provided to attend Bible school. I saw God meet my needs—spiritu-ally, emotionally, and physically. It was such a blessing to be in the perfect will of God!

Set Free

In January that school year I was sitting in class one day and all of sudden, I realized the grief regarding my husband was gone. Coincidentally or perhaps supernaturally, four of the people in our class were widows. Each of the widows in the class through hearing and sitting under the Word of God, listening to our instructor, and watching the Spirit of God move, were all completely set free of grief!

Prior to being set free, I would think of my husband and would miss him so much. When those thoughts came it would make me feel heavy inside because he wasn't there and I missed him so. He wasn't there to help me. He wasn't there to talk to me. He just wasn't there.

But that day in 2009 when I was set free from the emotional trap of the enemy, all of a sudden I could think about my husband and not feel the grief. I felt joy! I could remember the good times. I could remember the fun we had. What deliverance God brings to the broken-hearted! (See Luke 4:18-19.)

Keeping Perspective

I love my husband today just as much as I did when he was on earth. The love never goes away. I think that is so exciting! My mother gave me a great piece of wisdom after my father died. After being married more than 50 years, she would miss my father so much sometimes. She said it helped when she would start to think of the things my father did that absolutely drove her nuts. It brought her into reality and it got her back on track. Keeping perspective and moving out of the emotional into the good thoughts of God will keep you steady in the hard times.

Be encouraged even in the difficult hours. I know in the realm of our feelings and emotions, there are tough things to walk through. Know this: in Christ, the anointed One and His anointing, there is victory on the other side of loss and grief. As you bathe in God's Word so that it saturates you through and through, you'll find the victory belongs to you!

CHAPTER 8

Master Keys To A New Life

In this book we have not been seeking or looking for answers through man or the modern social system. The world system or man's answers simply coat problems but never really get to the heart of the real issues. God, through His Word and the Holy Spirit, has answers that empower and strengthen through every issue of life. He attacks root issues at ground zero. We don't want to just "cover" an issue but to confront and overcome the real problem. The following four master keys are God's answers for you. They are crucial for a victorious life: Salvation, the Holy Spirit, Prayer and the Word of God, and Other People.

Salvation

The first and most vital key to involving God in our lives is to connect to Him through the new birth or salvation experience. God has made provision for "whosoever shall call upon the name of the

Lord" (Rom. 10:13). Every answer to every problem in life is found in Jesus Christ, the Son of the living God, including where you will spend eternity. If you have never accepted Jesus Christ as your personal Savior, then you need to make sure you have taken that first step. Church attendance, good works, serving in church, and giving tithes are not going to get you an audience with Almighty God—only one thing is required: a personal experience with Jesus Christ.

If you're ready to get your life on an upward path toward divine aid and assistance—spirit, soul and body, then pray the prayer of Salvation and start a brand new life with God!

Holy Spirit, The Comforter

"Blessed be God, even the Father of our Lord Jesus Christ, the Father of mercies, and the God of all comfort; Who comforteth us in all our tribulation, that we may be able to comfort them which are in any trouble, by the comfort wherewith we ourselves are comforted by God" (2 Corinthians 1:3-4).

It is so amazing to know that our Heavenly Father is the God of *all comfort.* The Triune God—the Father, Jesus the Son of God, and the mighty Holy Spirit—come to dwell in us. Before Jesus left the earth, His early followers and disciples were sad when Jesus said He was leaving but He told them He was going to send *another* Comforter. This other Comforter is the Holy Spirit. Sending the Comforter was to the disciples' advantage because Jesus was housed in a flesh-and-blood body and could only be in one place at one time. But the Holy Spirit can be in everyone at the same time. Let's take a look at this mighty Comforter named the Holy Spirit that is available to you.

But when the Comforter (Counselor, Helper, Advocate, Intercessor, Strengthener, Standby) comes, Whom I will send to you from the Father, the Spirit of Truth Who comes (proceeds) from the Father, He [Himself] will testify regarding Me. (John 15:26, AMP)

We see this great and mighty Holy Spirit is a Comforter. In the Greek the word "Comforter" means Counselor, Helper, Advocate, Intercessor, Strengthener, and Standby.[4]

With this simple and brief look at the Holy Spirit, we can certainly see as widows we need this Third Person of the Trinity. I can attest to time after time where without the aid of my husband I didn't know what to do. But thank God for the Holy Spirit—the Comforter—Who would come and give me a Word, comfort or direction, whatever would be needed in a specific moment or situation.

Jesus was a Comforter to His disciples when He was here on earth, but we have such a great blessing with the Holy Spirit living *in* us through Christ. Knowing the Third Person of the Trinity—the Comforter—lives in us to give us the victory is something in which our faith can anchor. The disciples were challenged when Jesus told them He would be leaving (in the flesh). But if He didn't go the Holy Spirit could not come and dwell in each one of us. (See John, chapters 14-17.)

I had a situation happen in my family that I just didn't know how to handle or what to do. As I prayed the Lord told me to look up a particular Scripture. I looked it up and it had to do with relaxing and letting God take care of the situation. I had become pretty stressed and was certainly not trusting God in the matter prior to reading this Scripture passage. In the Message Bible, the Word was so very plain: "I, Jude, am a slave to Jesus Christ and brother to James, writing to those loved by God the Father, called and kept safe by Jesus Christ. Relax, everything is going to be all right; rest, everything's coming together; open your hearts, love is on the way!" (Jude 1). God's going to protect your children. It's going to be okay. It was a personal Word to me from the Holy Spirit. I could feel myself relax. I could sense a calm inside—the Comforter brought peace and comfort to me. He is there for all who call upon Him as Helper and Guide.

When you think of comfort you are normally thinking about emotional or physical needs, but the Lord can surprise you. A special moment of comfort for me—really, it was a thought-filled prayer that I never verbalized—occurred in the busy days of sorting through bills and the myriad of things to be done following Fred's death. In the midst of all these details I thought one day, You know what would be fun—*I just wish somebody I knew had a little baby. It would be fun just to hold a baby for a while.* I don't know why that thought came to me. I'm a grandmother!

My youngest grandchild was about three- or four-years-old at the time and so that was out of the question. I just thought it. It wasn't really a prayer. I didn't ask the Holy Spirit to send someone with a baby or anything. And I didn't know anybody who had a little baby. It was on a Thursday when I was just thinking that thought. I needed something different than all of the busy work I had to do.

On Saturday morning my daughter called me. At that time she was living next door to a single mom who had several children including a baby. The baby's aunt usually babysat for them on Satur-day mornings, but the aunt had become ill and the single mom needed someone to take the baby. So she asked my daughter if she would take care of the baby and she agreed. I didn't know all of this was happening. When my daughter called me about 9:30 or 10:00 in the morning, she said, "Could I come over and see you for a little while?" I responded, "Sure." We lived far enough away that it took her awhile to get there, maybe a half-hour.

When my daughter arrived she had this little baby with her. He was seven months old. He was one of those happy, cheerful babies, who just smiled and cooed and played. We put a quilt down on the living room floor and we just played with the baby. We just had so much fun that day, playing with the baby. I fed the baby and held him, while my daughter changed the diapers. I was blessed.

In the afternoon when he got tired, he just laid down on the quilt and went to sleep. None of my kids would do that! When he woke up he needed his diaper changed and a bottle, and then he played some more. I had that wonderful feeling of holding the baby, that joy of forgetting all my problems for a few hours, and that peace in relaxing and just having a good time. It may seem like a silly thing to a lot people but it meant so much to me. It was truly a comfort to me that the Holy Spirit, the Comforter, heard my heart one day and did it because He loved me. How wonderful is our mighty God. He sent a special moment to me just because He loves me.

Prayer and the Word of God

I've endeavored to give you God's Word regarding His answers and His perspective to widowhood. We definitely know an absolute key to victory over the challenges and grief we face as widows has to come from God's Word. As we read, meditate, and confess God's Word over the circumstances and situations we're dealing with from day to day, we will be strengthened, encouraged, and comforted to face our dilemmas and challenges.

Prayer is another master key, both as a supply for widows as well as a service to others. Especially in the New Testament we see the importance of widows participating in prayer for others. This applies to today's widows in the 21st Century Church. Prayer for others is another way that we move from our own feelings that sometimes try to consume us to becoming concerned with the needs of others.

One of the greatest ways to get our minds off ourselves is to pray for others. It's a way to get involved in others' lives and let go of our own concerns and self-preoccupation. Also, prayer for others is probably the greatest way to get our needs met. We often think about the passage in Luke 6:38 as a Scripture regarding getting physical or material needs met, but it says, "Give and it shall be given unto you...." That terminology has a wide range of applications. As we give prayer, then God returns it back to us "good measure, pressed down, and shaken together, and running over shall men given into your bosom." As widows we can pray!

Let's look at a great example of a praying widow in the Word of God from Luke 2:36-38. Anna, the prophetess, prayed for years in the Temple. In fact, the Bible tells us that she "served God with fastings and prayers night and day" (v. 38). She gave her life for others and had the opportunity to see Jesus as a baby. She immediately recognized Him as the Redeemer.

Another great example of a praying widow with persevering faith in Scripture is found in Luke 18. When we are looking to God to have our needs met, we have to persevere until we receive what God said belongs to us. This widow prayed for justice in a situation until the unjust judge finally gave her what she wanted. In verse 7-8 Jesus says:

And will not [our just] God defend and protect and avenge His elect (His chosen ones), who cry to Him day and night? Will He defer them and delay help on their behalf? I tell you, He will defend and protect and avenge them speedily. However, when the Son of man comes, will He find [persistence in] faith on the earth? (AMP)

One other well-known widow in the New Testament is found in both Mark 12:41-44 and Luke 21:1-4. When Jesus was looking over the offerings in the Temple, He commended the widow who gave two small coins out of her need: "This poor widow hath cast more in, than all they which have cast into the treasury: for all they did cast in of their abundance; but she of her want did cast in all that she had, even all her living" (Mark 12:43-44). Jesus commended her for the sacrificial offering she chose to make of her own free will, even though to others it was small.

So make your stand on the Word of God and stand in faith and in prayer for your own personal needs but also give yourself to pray for others. Out of love for the people who have been blessings to me, I spend time praying for them. I pray especially for other widows daily. That's something all of us can do. I pray for my children and grandchildren. I pray for my pastors, my church, and my nation. No matter what your circumstances as a widow, you can be used of God in one of the greatest ministries to the heart of God and accomplishment of Kingdom purposes—the ministry of prayer and intercession for others.

Other People

The last and a very important master key is other people. One of the greatest blessings in my life was other people that God most certainly sent to me in the beginning and God has also graced me with wonderful Christians who have become my lifetime friends. In this process of making adjustments and finding our place in life again without our husband, the encouragement and blessings of others both in material ways as well as spiritual are essential. Learning to appreciate and not become a burden to those women who will come into your life to help you is vital.

But God meets our needs many times through others. We are not an island unto ourselves or a Lone Ranger. We need one another! During this time of change, you will need to open the door to others—for your benefit—but also there will come a time to give out of yourself, step back into life again, and be a blessing to others. We are in this world for God's purpose and His assignment, and you can't do that alone!

CHAPTER 9

Scriptures To Pray

Promises Given by God for Widows

Exodus 22:22-24

You shall not afflict any widow or fatherless child. If you afflict them in any way, and they cry at all to Me, I will surely hear their cry; and My wrath will become hot, and I will kill you with the sword; your wives shall be widows, and your children fatherless. (NKJV)

Deuteronomy 10:17-18

For the Lord your God *is* God of gods and Lord of lords, the great God, mighty and awesome, who shows no partiality nor takes a bribe. He administers justice for the fatherless and the widow, and loves the stranger, giving him food and clothing. (NKJV)

Psalm 68:5

A father of the fatherless, a defender of widows, *is* God in His holy habitation. (NKJV)

Psalm 146:9

The Lord watches over the strangers; He relieves the fatherless and widow; but the way of the wicked He turns upside down. (NKJV)

Proverbs 15:25

The Lord will destroy the house of the proud, but He will establish the boundary of the widow. (NKJV)

Isaiah 54:4

Do not fear, for you will not be ashamed; neither be disgraced, for you will not be put to shame; for you will forget the shame of your youth, and will not remember the reproach of your widowhood anymore. (NKJV)

Malachi 3:5

"And I will come near you for judgment; I will be a swift witness against sorcerers, against adulterers, against perjurers, against those who exploit wage earners and widows and orphans, and against those who turn away an alien—because they do not fear Me," says the Lord of hosts. (NKJV)

Luke 18:1-8

Then He spoke a parable to them, that men always ought to pray and not lose heart, saying: "There was in a certain city a judge who did not fear God nor regard man. Now there was a widow in that city; and she came to him, saying, 'Get justice for me from my adversary.' And he would not for a while; but afterward he said within himself, 'Though I do not fear God nor regard man, yet because this widow troubles me I will avenge her, lest by her continual coming she weary me.'" Then the Lord said, "Hear what the unjust judge said. And shall God not avenge His own elect who cry out day and night to Him, though He bears long with them? I tell you that He will avenge them speedily. Nevertheless, when the Son of Man comes, will He really find faith on the earth?" (NKJV)

Blessings to People Helping Widows

Deuteronomy 14:29

And the Levite, because he has no portion nor inheritance with you, and the stranger and the fatherless and the widow who *are* within your gates, may come and eat and be satisfied, that the Lord your God may bless you in all the work of your hand which you do. (NKJV)

Deuteronomy 16:11-15

You shall rejoice before the Lord your God, you and your son and your daughter, your male servant and your female servant, the Levite who *is* within your gates, the stranger and the fatherless and the widow who *are* among you, at the place where the Lord your God chooses to make His name abide. And you shall remember that you were a slave in Egypt, and you shall be careful to observe these statutes. You shall observe the Feast of Tabernacles seven days, when you have gathered from your threshing floor and from your winepress. And you shall rejoice in your feast, you and your son and your daughter, your male servant and your female servant and the Levite, the stranger and the fatherless and the widow, who *are* within your gates. Seven days you shall keep a sacred feast to the Lord your God in the place which the Lord chooses, because the Lord your God will bless you in all your produce and in all the work of your hands, so that you surely rejoice. (NKJV)

Deuteronomy 24:17-19

You shall not pervert justice due the stranger or the father-less, nor take a widow's garments as a pledge. But you shall remember that you were a slave in Egypt, and the Lord your God redeemed you from there; therefore I command you to do this thing. When you reap your harvest in your field, and forget a sheaf in the field, you shall not go back to get it; it shall be for the stranger, the fatherless, and the widow, that the Lord your God may bless you in all the work of your hands. (NKJV)

Curses on People Refusing to Help Widows

Deuteronomy 27:19

Cursed *is* the one who perverts the justice due the stranger, the fatherless, and widow. And all the people shall say, Amen! (NKJV)

Job 22:9-11

You have sent widows away empty, and the strength of the fatherless was crushed. Therefore snares *are* all around you, and sudden fear troubles you, or darkness *so that* you cannot see; and an abundance of water covers you. (NKJV)

Isaiah 1:15-17, 23

When you spread out your hands, I will hide My eyes from you; even though you make many prayers, I will not hear. Your hands are full of blood. Wash yourselves, make yourselves clean; put away the evil of your doings from before My eyes. Cease to do evil, learn to do good; seek justice, rebuke the oppressor; defend the fatherless, plead for the widow. (NKJV)

Your princes *are* rebellious, and companions of thieves; everyone loves bribes, and follows after rewards. They do not defend the fatherless, nor does the cause of the widow come before them. (NKJV)

Isaiah 10:1-2

Woe to those who decree unrighteous decrees, who write misfortune, *which* they have prescribed to rob the needy of justice, and to take what is right from the poor of My people, that widows may be their prey, and *that* they may rob the fatherless. (NKJV)

Jeremiah 22:1-5

Thus says the Lord: "Go down to the house of the king of Judah, and there speak this word, and say, 'Hear the word of the Lord, O king of Judah, you who sit on the throne of David, you and your servants and your people who enter these gates! Thus says the Lord: "Execute judgment and righteousness, and deliver the plundered out of the hand of the oppressor. Do no wrong and do no violence to the stranger, the fatherless, or the widow, nor shed innocent blood in this place. For if you indeed do this thing, then shall enter the gates of this house, riding on horses and in chariots, accompanied by servants and people, kings who sit on the throne of David. But if you will not hear these words, I swear by Myself," says the Lord, "that this house shall become a desolation.""' (NKJV)

Zechariah 7:9-12

This is what the Lord Almighty said: Administer true justice; show mercy and compassion to one another. Do not oppress the widow or the fatherless, the foreigner or the poor. Do not plot evil against each other. But they refused to pay attention, stubbornly they turned their backs and covered their ears. They made their hearts as hard as flint and would not listen to the law or to the words that the Lord Almighty had sent by his Spirit through the earlier prophets. So the Lord Almighty was very angry. (NIV)

Matthew 23:14

Woe to you, scribes and Pharisees, hypocrites! For you devour widows' houses, and for a pretense make long prayers. Therefore you will receive greater condemnation. (NKJV)

Luke 20:46-47

Beware of the scribes, who desire to go around in long robes, love greetings in the marketplaces, the best seats in the synagogues, and the best places at feasts, who devour widows' houses, and for a pretense make long prayers. These will receive greater condemnation. (NKJV)

Malachi 3:5

"And I will come near you for judgment; I will be a swift witness against sorcerers, against adulterers, against perjurers, against those who exploit wage earners and widows and orphans, and against those who turn away an alien—because they do not fear Me," says the Lord of hosts. (NKJV)

Widows' New Covenant Responsibilities

Acts 6:1-5

Now in those days, when *the number of* the disciples was multiplying, there arose a complaint against the Hebrews by the Hellenists, because their widows were neglected in the daily distribution. Then the twelve summoned the multitude of the disciples and said, "It is not desirable that we should leave the word of God and serve tables. Therefore, brethren, seek out from among you seven men of *good* reputation, full of the Holy Spirit and wisdom, whom we may appoint over this business; but we will give ourselves continually to prayer and to the ministry of the word." And the saying pleased the whole multitude. And they chose Stephen, a man full of faith and the Holy Spirit, and Philip, Prochorus, Nicanor, Timon, Parmenas, and Nicolas, a proselyte from Antioch. (NKJV)

1 Corinthians 7:39

A wife is bound by law as long as her husband lives; but if her husband dies, she is at liberty to be married to whom she wishes, only in the Lord. (NKJV)

James 1:27

Pure and undefiled religion before God and the Father is this: to visit orphans and widows in their trouble, *and* to keep oneself unspotted from the world. (NKJV)

1 Timothy 5:1-16

Do not sharply censure or rebuke an older man, but entreat and plead with him as [you would with] a father. Treat younger men like brothers; [treat] older women like mothers [and] younger women like sisters, in all purity. [Always] treat with greater consideration and give aid to those who are truly widowed (solitary and without support). But if a widow has children or grandchildren, see to it that these are first made to understand that it is their religious duty [to defray their natural obligation to those] at home, and make return to their parents or grandparents [for all their care by contributing to their maintenance], for this is acceptable in the sight of God.

Now [a woman] who is a real widow and is left entirely alone and desolate has fixed her hope on God and perseveres in supplications and prayers night and day. Whereas she who lives in pleasure and self-gratification [giving herself up to luxury and self-indulgence] is dead even while she [still] lives. Charge [the people] thus, so that they may be without reproach and blameless. If anyone fails to provide for his relatives, and especially for those of his own family, he has disowned the faith [by failing to accompany it with fruits] and is worse than an unbeliever [who performs his obligation in these matters].

Let no one be put on the roll of widows [who are to receive church support] who is under sixty years of age or who has been the wife of more than one man; and she must have a reputation for good deeds, as one who has brought up children, who has practiced hospitality to strangers [of the brotherhood], washed the feet of the saints, helped to relieve the distressed, [and] devoted herself diligently to doing good in every way.

But refuse [to enroll on this list the] younger widows, for when they becomes restive and their natural desires grow strong, they withdraw themselves against Christ [and] wish to marry [again]. And so they incur condemnation for having set aside and slighted their previous pledge. Moreover, as they go about from house to house, they learn to be idlers, and not only idlers, but gossips and busybodies, saying what they should not say and talking of things they should not mention. So I would have younger [widows] marry, bear children, guide the household, [and] not give opponents of the faith occasion for slander or reproach. For already some [widows] have turned aside after Satan. If any believing woman or believing man has [relatives or persons in the household who are] widows, let him relieve them; let the church not be burdened [with them] so that it may [be free to] assist those who are truly widows (those who are all alone and are dependent). (AMP)

Titus 2:3-5

Bid the older women similarly to be reverent and devout in their deportment as becomes those engaged in sacred service, not slanderers or slaves to drink. They are to give good counsel and be teachers of what is right and noble, so that they will wisely train the young women to be sane and sober of mind (temperate, disciplined) and to love their husbands and their children, to be self-controlled, chaste, homemakers, good-natured (kind-hearted), adapting and subordinating themselves to their husbands, that the Word of God may not be exposed to reproach (blasphemed or discredited). (AMP)

CHAPTER 10

Practical Helps

Over the tenure of widowhood God has taught me some simple practical keys as well as spiritual helps to receive victory in every situation. Perhaps these keys will help when you're in one of those moments and you need to be quickly reminded, "Okay, I'm more mature than this." It's kind of like a Holy Spirit kick in the pants or the Holy Spirit nudging you in a way that only He can. Perhaps He is saying using current slang, *let's get over it! Get on with life! Get on with My plan for you! My abundance and blessings are waiting on you!*

Things to Do to Stay in Victory

- Read the Word of God every day.

- Have a thankful heart.

- Do random acts of kindness for others—a friend or stranger.

- Pray for those who bless you.

- Run (don't walk) to God when you are lonely—don't give the enemy a second!

- Meditate and pray the Scriptures daily for yourself and others.

Resist the Devil

- Beware of the devil trying to make you angry or unforgiving toward someone or God, or even your deceased husband.

- Beware of self-pity, unbelief, doubt, or why me?

- Beware of depression and grief opening the door to sickness after the death of a loved one. Don't let depression stay. Depression will be your enemy, not your friend!

CHAPTER 11

A New Day Dawning

It is my hope and prayer that as a widow, or a friend or relative of a widow, you have found some help. If nothing else, learn that the fears, concerns, or apprehensions you must face, you are not to face alone. There is a God in the universe Who cares and Who has solutions to help you through the journey of widowhood. There is life on the other side of the loss of a spouse. I want you to understand that one door has closed but God is opening another. You must see there is a new day dawning. As long as you hold on tightly to your hurt, grief, and sorrow, you will never find your way out of this dark place into the light of day—the place where God wants you to be.

God is there to help.

The Word of God is there to help.

People are there to help.

A moment will come when you will have to embrace the future. In Revelation 3:8 the Bible says, "See! I have set before you a door wide open which no one is able to shut" (AMP). We have to embrace a new journey and be willing to walk through it courageously as scary as it may seem. We began this book entitling it "Women of Courage." Of a certainty, it takes courage to walk through the darkness of this journey. But remember when Moses died and he was leading three million Jews into the Promised Land, He told his successor, Joshua, to do just one thing—be strong and of good courage! Obviously, it takes courage to be strong. And I tell you the same, it will take courage. But God is the source of that courage and He will not let you go or forsake you. You can come out on the other side in victory if you will decide to *go with God!*

In closing let me leave with you a Word of God from the Message Bible, Psalm 4:8. The Psalmist is talking about safety, peace, and sound sleep. He concludes with a great statement. I would like you to realize that God's desire for you is summed up in this verse:

"For you, God, have put my life back together."

Please know as you read, mediate, pray, and trust God with the Scriptures He has written just for you, *God will put your life back together again!*

Prayer of Salvation

Father, in the name of Jesus, I come to You recognizing my unworthiness of Your love and power. I have done nothing to deserve Your love and kindness. Yet, You love me just as I am.

I come to You in the name of Your Son, Jesus, acknowledging that Jesus died on the cross as a sacrifice for me. I believe You raised Him from the dead for my sin to make me a new creation. Therefore, I confess Jesus is my Lord, and I make Him Lord of my life right now.

Thank You for forgiving me of all my sin. Thank you for loving me so much. I acknowledge Jesus as Lord of my life from this day forth. Amen.

Prayer to be Baptized
in the Holy Spirit

Father, I am Your child, for I have believed in my heart that Jesus was raised from the dead, and I have confessed Him as my Lord.

I ask You now to fill me with the Holy Spirit. I step into the fullness and power that You promised in Your Word. Jesus, I ask You to baptize me with the Holy Spirit and with the evidence of speaking in other tongues. I confess I have received the fullness of the Holy Spirit and that I am a Spirit-filled Christian. As I yield my vocal chords to You, I expect to speak in tongues as the Spirit gives me utterance in the name of Jesus. Amen.

About the Author

Lynda Robinson was active in ministry with her husband Fred for many years before he moved to Heaven. She attended RHEMA Bible Training Center in Tulsa, Oklahoma in 1978, 1991, and 1992. After Fred's departure, she attended the DOMATA School of Ministry in Tulsa and since has been putting her training to work through ministry to widows. Lynda and Fred were married for 47 years and have two children and five grandchildren.

Endnotes

1 John Wesley, quoted from http://hopefaithprayer.com/prayernew/ prayer-quotes/, accessed April 30, 2012.

2 Jehovah Shalom. http://www.blueletterbible.org/study/misc/name _god.cfm#link16, accessed May 1, 2012.

3 http://www.biblestudytools.com/lexicons/hebrew/kjv/anah-4.html

4 Comforter. http://www.blueletterbible.org/lang/lexicon/lexicon. cfm?Strongs=G3875&t=KJV, accessed May 1, 2012.